refrain

Jason S Polley

refrain recounts the author's travels in India as an inexperienced and sensitive young man. The narrative shows wit, intelligence and a facility with words. The style is experimental and literary; and the fascination of the stories told – short stories in verse presenting the anxieties and misfortunes typical of shoestring traveling, and the culture-shock deriving from visiting a very different culture from ones own – carries the careful reader along. A knack for reading this less-than-conventional fast-paced book, which is at once humorous and nightmarish, passionate and detached, is acquired quickly.

Jason S Polley allocates his time to reading, scuba diving, practicing yoga, and getting tattooed. He began what was to become **refrain** in early 1997 while backpacking the Indian Subcontinent, but shelved it later that year to devote himself to the study and composition of academic prose. He returned to his lone work of fiction in order to meet the deadline for the 2009 Proverse Prize. Since 1998 he has lived in Guangzhou, Montreal, Bogota, Guayaquil and Hong Kong. He currently teaches American Literature and Culture at Hong Kong Baptist University.

refrain

Jason S Polley

Proverse Hong Kong

refrain

refrain
by Jason S Polley.

2nd pbk edition published in Hong Kong by Proverse Hong Kong, August 2016
Copyright © Proverse Hong Kong, August 2016.
ISBN: 978-988-8228-61-4
Available from https://www.createspace.com/6412757

1st published in Hong Kong by Proverse Hong Kong, 23 November 2010.
Copyright © Proverse Hong Kong, 23 November 2010.
ISBN 978-988-19321-4-3

Enquiries: Proverse Hong Kong, P. O. Box 259, Tung Chung Post Office, Tung Chung, Lantau Island, NT, Hong Kong, SAR, China.
E-mail: proverse@netvigator.com Web site: www.proversepublishing.com

Moral Rights: The right of Jason S Polley to be identified as the author of this work has been asserted by him in accordance with the Copyright, Designs and Patents Act 1988.

Cover photograph by Jason S Polley. Page design by Proverse Hong Kong.
Cover design by Proverse Hong Kong and Artist Hong Kong Company.

All rights reserved. No part of this publication may be reproduced, stored in a retrieval system, or transmitted, in any form or by any means, electronic, mechanical, photocopying, recording or otherwise, without the prior written permission of the publisher or publisher and author. The book is sold subject to the condition that it shall not, by way of trade or otherwise, be lent, re-sold, hired out or otherwise circulated without the publisher's or author's and publisher's prior written consent in any form of binding or cover other than that in which it is published and without a similar condition including this condition being imposed on the subsequent owner or purchaser. Please contact Proverse Hong Kong in writing, to request any and all permissions (including but not restricted to republishing, inclusion in anthologies, translation, reading, performance and use as a set piece or pieces in examinations and festivals).

Proverse Hong Kong
    British Library Cataloguing in Publication Data (1st edition)
Polley, Jason S.
Refrain : poems about a young man's experience in and of India.
1. India--Poetry. 2. Travelers--Poetry.
I. Title II. Bickley, Gillian
811.6-dc22

ISBN-13: 9789881932143

refrain

Everywhere you looked in India there was evidence of a past that had attained mythical heights. From philosophy to architecture, few civilizations have left such an awesome record. It was reputed to have made even the gods jealous of humanity.

— Paul William Roberts, *Empire of the Soul*.

refrain

refrain

Preface

The narrator of the linked stories in **refrain** is a Canadian ex-pat. He arrives in Delhi with a romanticized view of India, a pocketful of outdated maps, and a money-belt begging to be stolen. Rickshaws, buses, and trains take us through the ghettos as images filter through our ex-pat's sensibilities: we experience his battles with disgust and paranoia while moving through a rough and tumble city peopled by beggars, lepers, drug dealers, girls with "untied shoulder kissing hair," and swarms of destitutes. The savage streets make "sleep notpossible" and breed a "pynchon paranoia." What to do? Assimilate through self-reflection? Drive away fear by remembering "whitedevil pillage" and taking responsibility for the white man's greed? Yes. But he also realizes fear is a good thing because it takes him out of his comfort zone. Comfort limits the ability to see and to feel. The introduction of a "goodman...in avatar cleangreen sweater" offering help calms our ex-pat enough to realize this is indeed a city of contrasts, one where fleeting moments of safety can be found. And, sometimes, safety and danger collide. In 'distrust friendly gentleman', the narrator loses his pack to an apparent gentleman who distracts him long enough for his cohort to snatch it; but "unsmiling family man" helps him recover what was lost and warns him not to be taken in by locals who are too friendly.

refrain

In India, relying on first impressions can be dangerous.

Polley's technique of linking words, phrases, and dialogue creates a flow-of-thought that delivers urgent and intense impressions. This takes us along on a ride that feels cinematic, one jammed with sensory explosions that rock the sensibilities. It is as if the reader is pulled into the text itself to experience the chaotic, disordered images of India as they occur. This technique also creates fresh meaning. Buffaloes get "madviolent" and a "deadwhitemercedes" glides by, its passengers oblivious to the sufferings of shirtless men dodging traffic.

Our ex-pat will soon learn that western manners don't count and that "ukenglish" is a rarity. What does count is a "fistful of rupees" as he tries to adapt to an ever-shifting cityscape, one that makes room for the animals of the country: water buffaloes, cows, horses, dogs, and elephants. Fear keeps us grounded in the present. In 'textbooks yelltell truth', he says "three drivers must be plotting your demise" as his rickshaw zips toward Ringo Guesthouse and the driver admits "Englishnogood." The interior world is bombarded by new threats and powerful imagery as our narrator travels by public bus and train from cities to rural towns. In West Bengal's city of Darjeeling, he encounters monks, nuns, and white tigers. In the mountain borders we catch glimpses of Nepal, Tibet, Burma, and Bangladesh. There is

refrain

a sense that what India is today spills over those borders, for both good and for bad. In 'smile momentarily answers', we experience Gangtok with its lotus hotels, warm red rugs, stagnant thoughts, and the admission "dh lawrence is dead." Dead writers don't matter much to Polley because they've lived a separate reality and India's almost daily transmutations require the fresh eyes of a traveler.

The stories work as a sprawling dramatic monologue, one that encompasses numerous states and territories. Polley paints on a large canvas and his brush strokes are fresh, memorable, and cutting edge. And there is something more. You can open the book and start reading anywhere. In our expat's words, "it keeps on beginning."

Kirby Wright
Honolulu, Hawaii
Kirby Wright is author of *Punahou Blues* **and** *Moloka'i Nui Ahina*

refrain

For Denton; for Stephanie.

refrain

Author's Introduction

Maybe this jumbled collection of spontaneous fear and near-loathing re-re-collected thirteen years later in half-regretful semi-detachment, ought to be titled **run-on** rather than **refrain**. When I first visited India as a religious studies major in the winter semester of 1997 (I marked time in terms of semesters then, as I still do now), the place was for me an endless and unpunctuated run-on sentence. The novelty, noise, nakedness and aliveness, following hard upon the detoured and deferred touchdown of my first international flight, just never seemed to stop. On and on, those first 30 hours ran and ran, as I paranoically recount them in the opening piece "textbooks yelltell truth." Unordinary (to me) madness proliferated. I just couldn't compute or process India's context. The rules no longer applied. Nietzsche earnestly writes somewhere that he "fear(s) we are not getting rid of God because we still believe in grammar." Well, here I was, in India, a place once reputed to make even the gods jealous, and within minutes of retrieving my pack from the baggage track, the gods, not to mention grammar, were already long gone.

And so I fell into parataxis; I linked most of my, in retrospect, woefully multi-culturally-relative clauses, with *and*s. It was also as though I was at once experiencing the present and avoiding it. In the opening pieces of **refrain** I often turn to

refrain

other writers. I covertly allude to writers of India from the colonial period, including EM Forster, Herman Hesse, and Paul Scott. I also embed references to postcolonial Indian writers, like Salman Rushdie, Rohinton Mistry, and Upamanyu Chatterji. At the same time, I betray a weird sense of refuge (and/or rhetorical distance) when I refer to romantic distress (Thomas de Quincey and Charles Baudelaire), modern alienation (Franz Kafka and Joseph Conrad), and postmodern remove (Joan Didion and David Foster Wallace).

refrain begins by looking back, perhaps as a means to escape my first discomfiting impressions of India. Yet my addiction to allusion also speaks to a need to live in the future, to think myself forward to a retrospective time wherein I'm (amusingly? distantly? writerly?) recounting my First Travels in the Subcontinent. Was this feigned detachment an act of preservation? of escape? of grandeur? Or was it really about contemporary understandings of representation itself?

This India was not the one of textbooks; not the one of totalization, standardization, and canonization. This India commanded what was for me at the time a new sense of discourse—or at least one more patently connected to the formal experimentations and eyeball kicks of late high-modernism and early post-modernism. Form and content needed to be yoked, and the reader needed to be smuggled into the text. This is why my speaker uses the second-person; why he co-opts

refrain

"you," *you* the hailed reader.
    India gradually becomes less of a run-on sentence as I familiarize myself with the place, its people, and my position of super-privileged alterity. The later pieces of **refrain** illustrate this shift in the pendulum. I begin my travels as wide-eyed playgoer wishing I were squinty-eyed analyst. Yet as I continue to wander I do discover the grammatical ground beneath my feet; I do experience India in the present. Reining in my sentences and syntax while trying to preserve the innovation that India always-already heralds, I come to see India as a place not unlike any unknown other. It was, and still is two trips later, a place defined by what I've learned to appreciate as the positive wonders of disparity, difficulty, and desire.

Jason S Polley
Hong Kong
September 2010

refrain

refrain

refrain: table of contents

Preface by Kirby Wright	7
Author's Introduction	11
textbooks yelltell truth	17
coughed awake sudden	31
shivers shove eyelids	37
wide wide yatra	39
distrust friendly gentleman	41
darjeeling distance dream	45
platformpoint cloudy thin	49
smile momentarily answers	53
casual meander slow	55
buddhist beads explain	57
air india announces	61
as sure as	63

refrain

refrain

textbooks yelltell truth

textbooks yelltell truth
so three thrilling years india romanticized from classroom to classroom to classroom
and now livelong anticipated awaited stiff touchdown
   halfthree delhidarkness twentysixpointfive hours
   behind westernworld schedule
for fog in london means wine euphoria in
   paintbanlieured paris where french frenchalgerian
   frenchspanish frenchbasque female bone structure
breathesinstills stilllife in deadtired bigbeating
anxiousawake hearts that only want because four
wideopeneyes took
and thirdmap india where cartographic lines are neither
   authenticated nor correct
and long youve longed for goldentemple and tajmahal
   and brahmin uppercaste priestlyscholarly sannyasis
ultimately renouncing wordliness of it nonall
godly eyes alighting resting resisting
waybright saris saris saris
and Nai rickshaw dayonlysir
so dirtydark expensive Taxionlysir
and no dacoit stole your padded endlessly
   righthandpatted westernworld wallet yet
and shabby cabby points and parks on nowchristened
   shoulder enabling new driver to board
     as secreted nofare flops out mantra mumbling eyes
down hands hidden
and three drivers must be plotting your demise
and thoroughfares darklightless save for sometime
   glinting alloy of cycles dingdinging rickety past
and Nainai Nai atnight rickshaws klaxon racketfastpast
   always bleating beeping weeping
and drivers designate deputy to fastspeak
   Destinationnotpossible

refrain

though it was twenty minutes before
so
Ringo guesthouse Please
Notpossible
Rin go guest house Rin go Con naught place Rin go
    canada compulsory Please
Notpossible Englishnogood
and novel hotel Bestqualitysirs
puffingcoughingsnorting scantily clad scarf adorned taxi
    wallahs wantneeddeserve costly commission
and Norooms Nai hotel arrival
so multidrivered multidriven wayoffwhite1970something
    ambassador uncurbed and alreadytoobig packs
    burden knobbywobbly knees and Ajantahotel
    Bestqualitysirs
and balcony
and banging bunked destitutes down darklittered alley
    below bellowingloosing alreadylost lungs
kumbhakarna waking horns
dogs howl horrendousmadly
hazylazy holycows dismissivelydigustedly daring loud
    donkeys to desist
noise noise noise
whiter than whiter than whiter than white
and now halfive and 6800 people per square kilometre
    delhi starting to stretch awake stiff   cementforabed
bodies bugbitten with stomachs   that havent smelt seen
stuffed food since forever
and roomdoor does lock
check check check
and deeply scuffed tallboyportmanteau works as sentry
    blocking balconys thankfully thickdoor
and sleepings nogood
even after twentyfour hours on public plane and hours
    hours hours of parisian curlicued queues
    punctuated by finewine wobbles
sleep notpossible

refrain

eyesmindbody unstopping
and pynchon paranoia panic popsperseveres
and wantneed to stopsteal away minds
    buildingbreakingcomparing weaving whying
    abilitydefficiency endlessly pointlessly
youve not read about this
two hours of neverestful respite wrestling
    wonderingwandering
and that cursed litterlane nomad cant have lungs nor
    larynx left to coarsecough nomore
and dogs may have gained the tallboyblocked balcony
    and traffic chaos so loud it savagely wakes
    sadsighing sun
and first subcontinent shower shivered coldly closes dirt
    and winedark plugged pores
and balcony view cursescompelscatapults you to hide all
    over again
and second person facilitates separation distantiation for
    the i eye ay cant be seen while seeing
touched while touching
hit while hitting
read while reading
recognized while orientalizing
you a falsely innocentignorant rhetoricalremoval alibi
nai
nai
nai
ay ay ay
and buildings stacked on breaking buildings twisted   rebar
reaching everywhichwhere
and everythings not westernworld red and green
and lookawayduckquicknow dirtcaked Baksheeshbaba
    kid below might perceive you right through top   of
heavyhead while fondling finds in heaps below   to
salvagesellrecycle
to live yet another deadlong day
and maimedblamed dogs suddenquickchew sludge and

refrain

    yelpingly avert barefoot ribcracking lungsucking
    quickkicks
and cow crosses forever narrowingclogging alleyartery
    with rickshaws whizzing peddlingbelling fastpast
and after constantly contemplated resounding white   noise
rattlehum mantra of the 747 downtown delhi aggravates
ears to bursting so long
after so little
time
time
time
and birds own tree and kids kids kids below across
    cement choked compound dirtyhealthymile away
    at universal marbles
and quickdownduck as anyguyoneguy onearm oneleg
    onetincan divines eyes from up thereby reaiming his
maybe evenlycurious twoeyed gaze
and this floor four
and doors locked
rerechecked
and big tallboy scraped back on silent shiftduty
and
and straddling stirring street head hollering hollow trying
    to blend casualcool with racing ravenous fasteyes
    unblinking stretching monstermouth and
    perpetually pivoting needmoreperipheral neck   and
shiny blue shoelaces bottoming everlankier   legs
roarrun rickshaw desperate dodge
and dustfree mercedes disparity
and realbrighthot sun
and overstepping stillblanketed hopefully stillbreathing
    bodies
and piles of red orange yellow blue indigo violet green
    refuse and mules and water buffalo and goats and
    kids and kids and dogs cows pigs horses animal   farm
and wallahs offering Rickshawbaba and the tin or
coppercan trinity Baksheeshbaksheeshbaksheesh and shops

refrain

and taxis grabbing at eyes and billfolds and
    innocentnefarious white mercedes hornroar   smoothly
fastpast
echoing the two echelons
and you
you
you bustback to bestworstqualityhotelsir hotel
    heavenandhell after brusque offhand horror to
    regroup pulsing mind to fear and trembling
    feelingsweavings of whitedevil pillage
white privilege
another deadwhitemercedes spotlessly effortlessly glides
    fastpast
so
in other direction and dark narrow neverstreets with
    people unshaven shirtless wanting
and dodging rickshaws
but give holycows right of way
and water buffaloes can get madviolent
and not from meat
and No Nainai
fuck customary canadiancortesia pleasethankyou as   fistful
of rupees shuffling lady forces red badges   of ignorance
onto stillshiny shirt   Baksheeshbabiesschoolnow
Nainai Nai
and rip rawhands forcefast weave upout quickduck fast
    parting dread sea of rickshaws and No Nai Nai til
    tongues redraw from slapping teeth and mouthtop
    halfandhalf
and goodman looking thirty in avatar cleangreen sweater
    materializes Can i helpyou
and names latif and somethings sensitivesensible and buys
chai followed by hotel transfer to   cleanercheaper and
performingparanoia presumes   since cleangreen latif aged
twentyone much   toonice but cant offend
so bond not broken and buy him lunch and menu leads to
    comments on somehow coincidental kashmir

refrain

and the travel agents only a block away and pretty
    pictures white mountains and soft snow solicits   an almostunweary smile
delhis noisesmelldirt disappearing
and price steep but faux politesse forcedcoerced to go
    and cant offend firstfriend so travellers cheques
    signed and spent
and novel news
Youleavenow
We thought sunday
Betteryouleavenow Tonight
We need sleep
Yousleep Vanverytoomuchgood
Sleep we needing Very much
Noproblem Bestqualitysir Van gonow
less than kind
so two day today premature sign out from prepaid hotel
    as right hand writes lie about destination so
    lesscleangreen latif wont lose commission
in toomuchgood van and bumper to bull to shop to stall
    to pounding pedestrian to crawling and limping   lepers
to ancients inhaling hazy opium to dead dogs to hapless
horses to overweight overwait elephants to armless man
aiming stump through   window in hurried holy hope
Baksheeshbaba   Bababaksheesh begging
and His arms bustedbroken off His arms off His arms
    fucking busted off
and madness and mayhem and fear and loathing and
    trembling and shock and awe fills van windshield
another tv screen
and horns hollering Baksheeshbegging trapped traffic
    until a piledhigh house stacked sixseven layers up
    and on another floorfour and latifs cousins
    grandparents friends neighbours take turns   sleeping
on the cold hard concrete in seeming   jewish mourning
greywhite wool blankets breathing
coals gifting heat

refrain

in the heat
you sit on a dustybrown madeup mattress as sun sets
    oranging offwhiteyellow unflat flats and kashmiri
    chai collectschippers latif
laughing
urging
Yourest Iget hashish
and rest robbed of relax
and in india at someones humblehouse and noise nullifies
senseandsensibility amplifies   prideandprejudice
cantwont sleep
fear of stolen backpacks broken backs and brain
    bombarded body running relentless endless eyes
    always peeled
and an enfattened kurtz would be running the show by
    now
de quincy and baudelaire opiated pupils dilated
didion an unspied spy a triaged list
foster wallace a new tshirt
and green shivalatif returns hash handhidden blue van
    begging you allaboard and road traffic
    tiresomedeadly
and confined to delhis kafka castle weaving bleeping
    slipshawing starving slowfast past lorries lorries
    lorries
and Blow horn and Use dipper at night bluepaint backing
    thousands upon millions of wild orange goods
    carriers
and finally forget twelve million desperatedisparate
    countrycapital delhi
and highways a country road without country bumping
    passing slumping on and still still people spilled
    everyallwhere
and culture shock hits attacks stumbles and stuns
    flashing back filmreel real to lady looking twenty
    but probably old at twelve that baksheeshed your
    ghostly fortunate fortune rich skin Baksheesh

refrain

>Baksheesh block after packed block after blurred
>block black water loudlicked by dogs and people
>unharmoniously lepers losing the sisyphean streetrace

Specialservicesir
and another indexed now screening and screaming
>differences you werent taughttold to see
ideologically to be
and its duskdark
and score after score of smoky blaze along hazyhighway
>each fire now another runon sentence   illuminating
mounds of human beings grazing   gazing old metal
rippedstripped trucks stripped slowly
memory a palimpsest of masking palimpsests
and stop to eat
restaurant dishwasherwallah squattingworkingsinging in
>garbagejuice a mere metre away from openworld
>litterlatrine
so food no
Naiway
runreturn to van wary to be seen or left alone or
>accompanied or thoughtcriming
and eyes finally weighted down mind dumbnumbing
perchance to dream
and doors instantly open wide and denton and drivers
three again
always three
indias secular trinity
and doors slam shut and bulky blanket wrapped on warm
and drivers want hazylazy hashhugs from the tolaten
>grams denton franticforced scored from shivalatif
and cant offend
and it may help secure sleep
so inhaled and fastexhaled not giving it givego grabgift
>chance
to laugh or not to laugh
whether tis nobler
and fires and high beams constant colliding flashes

refrain

    overtake tumbling trucks and traintracks and
    headondeadon eyesclosed brakes shouting
    accidentsavoided again and again and again
and textbooks obsolescence
and always people
whiteeyes building flames
and brain buildsconstructs a kashmiri conspiracy
and where are you
and need second person separation
and now theres army announcingaskingimploring
    diviningconspiring
and drivers thrustingrustling murdered rupees into
    uniformed halfhappy hands
and everyones in on it
and paranoid delusions illusions elusions illuminati
    allusions control the trip persuade perspective   and
these guys are truly wise and stop for chai   and
moneybeltvisa verified passport memorised I   L 23 23
23 I L 23 23 23 IL 23 23 23 money tucked into sweatsick
sweatsock and these guys got us good and travellers
cheques checked and are you really kashmirvalley
vehicled
and bestfriend dear denton may be delving into this too and
this denouement
and moneybelt touched and tightened and punjabi
    boarder guards bullshitted and baksheeshed away
        and sixhour paranoia pulsing building and   victorinox
knife knuckled in sweatslippery   soaked hand and tears
stopperedstifled and not   letting the eyes get lazy
lackadaisical and sleepless for fourdays a detriment
reason deprived
winedine in nostalgicparis weakened
and starveddevoured energy bar neither hits nor helps
just haunts
speak nor use daggers
get thee
Latif

refrain

We have friends Who trek in two years Maybe you
    perhaps Can be good guide improvised fabricated
    dissembled to longerlast your lives
and thoughts think conspiracy controls
    tyrannytorturetreasontrip and highway   hallucinations
and stop for fuel
and dad is dialed
never make known
and antic informal normal
Yeah, its crazy
But yeah Im just real fine
and nose not sniffed
and kashmiri driverscompanions frantic rushyou
    pushyou from phone
and long grey hair longer grey beard phone stand man
    hopes to help because guest is god in
    incredibleindelibleindia
but he the godly
and edgyantsy almost drop knife and dentons
    sweatyshaky goosebumped touchy too and must
    abstain but smoke drivers flyhigh to have fighting
    chance at change
but denton dutifully lost black stone for army alarms and
    scandals scare and kashmiricustoms crossed army
    alleviated
and long lies for Toomuchgoodminivan private not
    public transport and stomach begs baksheeshes   about
twentyhour fast seeing sun whisper salaam   slowly and
army everywhere in jampacked   wintercapital jammu
and its holyhilly slipshaw sloped and big rock boulders
block and blur   indian army sandbag scenery
and seven am scary dismount dropoff and a driver needs
    Baksheesh Tipforme
and you are chatterjees agastya marvelling at roadside
    vegetable and fish shops sugarcane juice stalls   being
set up at seventhirty in the morning from   the gate
shacks seemed to stretch to the horizon where glinted the

refrain

silver of the river the shitting   children got up to thump the
car as it passed as if   egging it on at a rally
and all amazed at whitefright pale staring
    reachingtouching and lookwantwish to leap into a
releasing rippingrickshaw to greatescape being   pillaged
pointblank here as some   lonelyladyhearts prays loud eyes
no longer empty   pointingposturingperforming
and people people people toasting sunrise surprise
and what about plushlushpagodas and ornate temples and
    austere monkmanaged monasteries and imams
    megaphoned messages
and it just keeps on ending and into small bus and your
    seats are stolen so head back to the secondfromlast
bumpy back and dont talk or even   breathe
and entire entourage vacuums up staring
    silentamazedawed at clear lack of colour
at hollowmen seeing hollowmen seeing hollowmen
    seeing hollowmen
and shakingshivering scaredscarred eyes erased   trembling
and the infamousthey plot cunningly   for
privilegedespised demise unspeaking
and madness moves and victims evacuate but dont
dont
dont
strangers starving stares surround bus all wanting a part
    of potent plot and howl howl howl
and cant relaxreposerest
eyes everywhere full of unansweredunredeemed rewards
    and moneybelt secretly reswiftly secured
and trembling knees wont settlestop
and bus starts ascent so pack must be stolen golden gone
    into the underwonderworld with ravanalatif
and blanketed moneybelt brushed and denton tucks
    hiddenbefore tola deeper into stretchedsock and
    stashcash still secure ankleknuckled
and twistingwindingclimbing vessel a vacuum except for
    racing molested mind menacedmusing trying to

refrain

      unfold surrounding delusional conspiracy and
      artfully able to decipher every english punjabi
      kashmiri urdu syllablewordsentenceintention that
      speaking meanman oneseatoverandback yellcasts
      loud jocomocking your every eyewink   neckrotation
coldsweatwhitebrowipe
and hear a litanymantra that begins and ends
      Whitepassportvisamuchmoneygora
and miniscule monkeys sit still staring on brown
      roadtrailside boulders providing foreground to   grass
househuts pastoral paysans tea plantations   and himalayan
foothills and endless rockyride will stop with stolen
passports money love life
and meanman yelltelecastor points and youre outsider
      gaze just murders
and windows watch waiting for you to launch down
      clapping cliffs into vivacious void arms crossed
too too sullied
and stall for foodbreak and chest pneumonic from new
      cold and restless sleepless foodless frail fightingfigure
disposessed
and dont surrender your eyes
and overly occupied horrified mind
and back on bus
on bus or off bus
and mcmurphy could cope neithereither
chief broom an invisible man documenting
cassady counting
and the tunnel to true kashmir valley makes moneybelt
      more sore
and bus broadsided by militarys must to bust brave
      militants
so baggage scanned
and is your pack still atback and denton suddenstands
      struggling for escape
and yellcaster talks and stalks
and both forcedpushed back and army aims bus

refrain

      inandthrough tunnel tightfisted racing redhot
      deadtired humbled heart five arteries fighting
      pumping on not strong enough but long enough   to hit
snapcoldsnowstorm truekashmirvalley and   down down
deep down to topsyturvy tip military   curfew
commanding martialawliving random   strike day dwelling
kill shoot bang think walk in   groups of three
indiacontrolled kashmiri summer   capital srinigar
bunkers everywhere
flames fanning
warning
and kanata is to india what india is to kashmir
and bus stops and people passengers disappear
your baggage
your being
and moneybelt checked knife squeezed and stand up and
      exhausted fall sideways on two kashmiris that   never
surrender silent squintfree stare
Um sorry Legs too long for the womb
voice cracks but wit doesnt
ever
and hailhit the rickshaw coughcold and houseboat home
      maybe since baggage is on your back and indian army
armed and rickshaw relaxes and dont bother bettering
bartering
and onto cikara
but water dark and snow steals reflection of stars
and leap off knees knockingknowing onto maze of
      weeping wood bending brave under   westernweight
and its ramaddan
and houseboats warm and kashmiri chai kept waiting with
firesinging woodstove and rice and curry   expands
shrunkenshriekingsavouring stomach
inshallah
and water bottles in big blanketed redbed bedroom
      burning woodstove holyhot
dal lake freezes

refrain

you melt

imams echoes answer

refrain

coughed awake sudden

coughed awake sudden six am
stuff stuffed packingup packs
but small breakfast for bumpybus to jammedjammu
Sukrya sukrya Salaammailekum Maleikumsalaam
maharaja wallet weeping hospitality Baksheesh

and cikara labours blade thin ice speaking skywinedark
bus boarded eyes silent luggage lugged Uptop
kashmiri camouflage cangri panchu watchingkeeping
    warminghiding you
jammu twelvehourslikedays away

and dalailama dharamsala athenacharioted tomorrows
    tomorrow

and bus stops frequent
oneway track twoway today
and bigbreakingscreamingorange transporttruckred shiva
    yellinghollering
and loaded bus ahead topples overdown inviting
    grandgorge
silent

and pushedoff bus runquick
passports padded visas verified forms filled
rising sun singingsinge
and bus steepsteps slow
wide widowing trucks passenger petite cars burst past
and mountain foodstall stop

and bigpated trenchcoat hunchback of untouchable
    damecaste
bigboil shadinghiding left alwaysblackeye
and spits you away

refrain

moneyed mirage
and raspyrude commandingdemanding Baksheesh no Baba
panting bus sits waitingsilent
and starter turnschurns trudging desperate

sun screaming sweat
and camouflagetoque hot
and joyce starts stephens second story climactic
and monkeys stare too
and green oasis onehundred bodies down sucks sun
and ride worms forevertime
so eyes swindled to restrest
but tired sun whispering secretsslow bleeding littleleft
    snow crimson

and happyhimalaya red reminds of yesternights indian
    republicday dal lake bomb blast that sent hearts
    stutterstumbling eyes widewaking ears   hellbelling
bodies ninetydegree elling headcaved   pillows waiting
and twelve civilians to cemeterysymmetry
and now army armed everywhere
now capital jammu stretching closer in dreaded
    darkdistance
and moons not close enough to metempsychosis
and a ninethirty weary darkdismount and Nainai Nai the
    bus conductor cant have your bags clothes shoes smile
inevitable crowd congregating
invisible hands supplicating
handling grasping wanting needing dying
and you wonder about randomhaymakers
    insidecombinations lead ribcrackingrights
and Bestquality
Hellofriend
Hotelrickshaw Bustrain
Baksheeshbaksheesh Baksheesh

and Nainai Nai and army frisks missing hash and

refrain

    postlapsarian samaritans eloquence erasedeffaced
    as bunk bordertax commanded demanded secured
but dalailamas dharamsala destination bus departing
    luxurious real for four bumpyblocks
until it stalls and stops
Youstaybus
blanket tossed conductor driver passengers longgone
and army knocking quizzingneeding
denton relievingproviding
and moonstars suck suns expiring energylatency shock
    shiverquiver
dreams undreamt

and six am bus unparks
himachal pradesh border loomingblooming bigsmiles
and lineups lived
and militarymercenarymilitant jammukashmir
    disappeared by quickbright lightloud smiling sun

and near stareless foodbreak
but fastpaststuck hands still troubletremble eyes   dartdoubt
heart startstop for fastfrisks   toppedtempted with
realrapid difficultdigress   querriescomments
and startled stares linger longpast mapmakers
    blackborders
and bus stretches on long and suns paleorange streaks
    rest then rustrub away to daily babyblue
and suddenquicknow persuadedpushed from rolling bus
and wherewhere

and lope back bangingbusting bus doors to grab glowing
    going neargone gear
and no bus station herewhere
and tintedglass aircon covered agent answers announces
    Dharamsala Bestqualitytaxi 800 rupeesir
Government busstand Weneed
700 Rupeesir

refrain

Wewant Busstand
Foryou 600rupeesir Toomuchgoodprice Sir
and directions demandeddemandeddemanded
and city bus found and shoulders hug saggingceiling packs
bulkilybashing backs heads souls and   alleyes
gapingagape and government bus stand stumblestopdrop
and Baksheesh Baksheesh Baksheesh ring of handshearts
reachinggreeting but unwalletanswered so karma
triplecursed evil
but hope born big as reallive widewide smiled tibetans
     greetbow Namaste

but twentysix january republic day
so banks break
travelers cheques uncashable useless
but transport
bed
hunger
heat
heart
and Baksheeshbaksheesh redenied
and karmic curses unlifted invoked
and speciousprecious bunk bordertax relamented
and todays tomorrow

and everysingleone handles stares squints sniffs your
     travellers cheque
world dictateddetermined by eyesquinting authenticating
     connoisseurs
and stationmanager pipestem points you from his
     premises for smoking
and Baksheesh Baksheesh
and Youcomebackhour
and Nai taxi Nai
600rupee Bestqualityonlysir
and Nai and temper testing hunger hankering light
     dimming fear fostering

refrain

and dharamsala peaceful exile mystic mountain haven
   minilhasa awaits five everlonger hours away
and dalailama desperation denied as bus is   Fortyrupeessir
not the misdisinformed Twohundredonlysirmadam
so tickets ticketed karma baksheeshed bus boarded
and poshpolish girls gracing long lightbrown carefree
   caressing resting untied shoulder kissing hair
   addressed
and camouflagetoque pockethidden
and fear erased breath regained hope retained life
   remained

refrain

refrain

shivers shove eyelids

shivers shove eyelids up
breaking seal abrupt
ending fireplace dreams
to smell of smiling sun
hiking himalayan ridgerange

brand newborn days rays
misty mystic mountain snow rock
and open torii gate guesthouse door
reveals curious never idle youthful eyes
and burgundy robed buddhist nun

heart tempo upbeat quick triple take
doorways not a tv screen
holy answer above words solace silence
and orange sky creeps up up no fade
nun floats up open roof cement wall hall

to suns light orange breath rays
you follow contemplating contentment containment
and small neat tidy tight green carpet
two tiny beds small black stove
grey fading peeling chipping wood table

one hundred yearyoung learned learning lama
and motions sit alongsidebeside
and glowing knowing nun pours
big black thermos tea topping smile to smile to smile
and your mouth bigger stilleyes unclosing unblinking

refrain

and sins rememberedabsolved
and cinematic real guru sits
swollen strong hands shifting prayer beads
silent mouth mantra meditating
and big black thermos retipped repoured

ceramic cups all the way up
and clear white towel absolves
and Thankyou Sukrya
and silence laughs past language limits
and unbeginning unending smile

and butter thick kicks tasty tea
and her eyes give give great great
classrooms quickly erased
and lama handles your big black
buddy holly woody allen henry rollins eyes

wisdom smiling mouth mantra muttering
and nun big deep brown slow squint
her real renouncing black hair shaven
holy head dips down
shaking side to side to side

and mouse rests on your untouchable toes
and lama mouths slowly surely Merica
Canada and makeshift midair cartoon map
and oats gruel crunch chew stomach
starting heart happy eyes busting widening more

tricked taste buds undesiring unsuffering
and laugh laugh laugh emptinessfullness
and door lama hand body mind strong
and sun drips sweat
and himalayas breathe snow slow

refrain

wide wide yatra

wide wide yatra car festival jagannathjuggernaut
pilgrimagers pilgrimaging endless soundless
chai shops clothes shops juice shops book shops
saffron stained barelyloved lepers tincans clanking
pale dead body hoisted crazycovered orange green
yellingyellow deadred draped breathing flowers
exgrey feet hangingdangling painted proudloud pastel
furious bulls cheer snapping horns hard
and Rickshaw rickshaw Rickshaw bigbells beating
nagging leper singlearm elephantiasis sannyasi

singleframe

refrain

refrain

distrust friendly gentleman

distrust friendly gentleman who says Sit relax and Put
    pack uptop and then appears outside your train
    window and tells you to open it wide for its Very hot
humid
and you talk about canada and germany and his Germany
    girlfriend and the Six languages he knows and his
    Bad english intonation and his 86 graduation and
    he says thrice Light you have
and you dont so the unsmiling family man in the seat
    beside grudgingly passes out his butt through   black
barred window
and conversation continues as friendly gentleman walks
    back fading into justpostdusk trainstation   platform
darkblackness
and you bring him back lightning alive by quoting the
    conversation with returned mineral water in hand
    biscuits in other denton who then suggests a game of
chess to Burn some time
and he reaches above for the board in his pack as you
    stand and look above eyes emptying and thank   the
god of the hour after touching glasses patting
    moneybelt
and you miss your journal and novels for they were
    sleeping in your pack which is now running on   the
back of conniving conspiring disappeared   friendly
language gentlemans accomplices   unseen longgone
quickcrafty hands
eye desperate frantic to find starving search follows as
    train tells you look up and down absence echoing   it
wont be found

you ask frowning cigarettebutt familyman about houdinied
pack
and his eyes go wide as search party grows by one to three

refrain

and he leads you off the train owleyed head
    fumblingstumbling incredulous
and his eyes grow glowing hand raises index finger
    shooting and his mouth follows
Run runrun Go go Gonow trying to keep up with his legs
    and the canter conveys coloured hope ahead and you
exhale instinct alone and familiar green and purple on grey
platform in black night in front of   red train and mouth
pops as the friendly language   gentlemans unseen before
accomplice quick   pivots eyes stopping mouth waiting
you wonder loud What are you doing times three and
    unsmiling family man pants out questions index
    triggering target as the friendly language
    gentlemans thieving accomplice stumbles on   truth
and drops pack down drastic and then points   and
hesitates the way to the locomotive almost   holy buddhist
bodhgaya bound and steps into one cars side and shoots
through the other and his   walking lead becomes a sailing
slippery getaway down the steelline
you stunnedrelievedsaved by the regained weight down
    spine adrenaline adapting
and unsmiling family man wails Polizei Polizei Polizei
    to invisible beige uniforms that wont be german and
youre dumbfounded dumb and the   inevitableincredible
india crowd congregates and   coagulates round you and
frowning family man and hindi oriya fastlow english
explanation   replays that would amazenchant maybe
    startlestifle the chronicling fingers thumbs ears of
    faulkner and clemens
and sweaty shiver shaking burden and big glee in bloated
    loaded mind
and all you want to do is hug the unsmiling family man
    who never liked the friendly language germany
    girlfriend bad english intonation 86 graduation
    ungentleman from the getgo as quakingquivering
    body delivers him pale thinning deadwhite right for
trinity time

refrain

and he You verylucky Youverylucky and leading pulls
   you past constantlycurious crowd back to car as   you
hide smile from eye wanderingwondering   denton
and you place your biggerburdennow bag on hook
   knowing there are light bulbs watching and surer
   plots pondered and This is india

and comfort of three minutes previous stakes you breaks
   you makes you

refrain

refrain

darjeeling distance dream

darjeeling distance dream
and mahayana monks meditating
negating nodding knowing

and eightyyearyoung nun
handhumbling bigbow touchfeet
threeday wellingdwelling Namaste Sukrya

and baksheesh beggers
temple temple temple bodhgaya greatgates
Juicenowaternoice

and fiftysomething bighair white
and Are you buddhist
and Om mani padme aums the chastepace passing monks

and his hotels Tiptop topnotch
and hes Bombed from travel
and executes Easy new york exorcisms

and wears Armani threads
and lived Renouncing real
comforting coldcave two yawning years

and a Major monk eight springsummerfallwinters
and Rocknroll a twentyear allstar career
and pocket packs thick greenback for comforts crime

and Samapatti samadhi buddhism
and Failures of castesystem hinduism
and traffics in Goddamned truth

refrain

and never commits errors mistakes oversights
and not just The guru of new york
and Watch out for them wallethirsty tibetans

and Sit your ass down and meditate
I was there I was there I was there
and Go see supramysticaltranscendental cosmic conscious metempsychosis darjeeling bodhisattva awesome all altruist

and Treat yourselves to fivestar windemyre
Drink johnny walker special by librarys fire
and Listen to fiveman string quartet

For its a touch damp in darjeeling
and hes determined by females
and forgets crystal water on tired table

and horning hoarding cyclerickshaw gaya trainstation
    bound
and blackblue buffalo zebrahorns rub dentons arms
    realredraw
and broken buildings grey gripping grabbing eyes

and dead rats camus pneumonic bubonic
plague you other desperate direction
and Friendbaksheesh Namaste Friendstop

and allaboard patnapointed line
and samaritan slides you a slippery seat
indown squeeze inverting frown upsidedown

and denton will bustbreak rubberbend neck
sleeping slipping sway snap
and trains ticksticktickticktktktkts drastic discontinue
and photo album reveals college tall certainsmiled
    samaritans sister

refrain

whom you should meet marry carry burry
and 92 kilometres in six hours

and you walk last two
aggressive sun saluting loudly
and cycle rickshaw kickshaw smashcrash

cigarettes as swords wielding piercing screaming
and coarse horse roperubbed bloodneck crooked cart
pedestrian pollution market shop beggar patna

and delightful journey ersatzluxury bus leaves now
and shoved toughtimes back bouncing tail bench
and sun sets squinting silent

dark crusade corridor shifty eyes shaded shops
and juveniles jump luggage ladder
and prized heavyburden packs uptop

and onearmed lear gloucester fusion conductor screams
    revenge
roof squatters banished bus wheels round and round
and pitstop no water no bath no comfort

and sweat serious serious sweat serious serious
and thirsthink tall dripping foam nearslush ale
and monks gift holy clean cold quenching thumsup cola

and caffeine catapults losthighway hallucinations
and one am quiz with thirteenyear youngancient
and White tigers dare Darjeeling

refrain

and Watch out being cheated You unfamiliar
and God writes in your open palms
and sun sleeps alone then screams fiery salaam salutation

and flirty thin clouds tease tint touch trespass sunfire
and beadflaying loudsinging lifegiving monk loudlaughs
and time talks bus stops toes stretch legs lengthen

and no kneeroom no neckroom miniminibus
and shoulder clavicle neck head redent banged top
and burly conductor bawls and bus obeys briefly

and half the fares flutter without
and doppelganger conductorleadman trade
and siam must make more sense

and toy trains centenary line
130 bisections intersections perplexions
large lazy loops road crisscrossing

and transmission bleeds road pinkpurple
and navy uniformed students bus Baksheesh
and where the white tigers

and emphyzema man crazy coughs smoke spirit soul
and Speed thrills but also kills
and We want gorkha land
and denton crazycrackneck near split
sleep sweep sway snap weep
and station steel rods talkpoint running clouds

and mountain cold steep twisty walk enlivens
and lazy sunset lingers long
a happy crimson forever fever

refrain

platformpoint cloudy thin

platformpoint cloudy thin foam ganesh tok tourist temple
and almost overcast view
bhutan southeast
occupied tibet northeast nepal west
burma and bangladesh himalayahiding southeast
and sikkim

and incredibleincredulable india everyallwhere and   heavy
prayer flags restingrelaxing

little brown postprepubescent puppy shakes paw blanketing
bent legs in bur fur and starved sand

and seven k away dzoonga restaurant one floorup and
    wallet will thin
and male caucasian doublenosering plaidpants big
    blackboots and unending knotty deaddredded
    ropehair sits silent displeased alongside
    doublenosering onelipring midback   bruisingbrown
dirtydreds unsmiling unspeaking   caucasian female

and midsize houndpuppy ventures slow at foodfilled
    brown bowl owned by small overabused wornout
    grey mopmutt unmoving on browncushion   couchbed
and puppy creeps cautiouseyes snoutdevouring jaws
    jabgrabbing mopmutts suntanning mashed   ricecorn

and caucasian doublenosering male and postmodern
    retroromantic cash register and dreddedhair
    talentwisted touching lowback of plaidwrapped   knees
and accent maybe ukenglish
voice wax all reed
no sham
louder so too swelling manner of wellspoken

refrain

    mayorcortesia sikkimese restaurant managerproprietor

  and mopmutts old blueeyes mangy discord face yelping
    yap yells and brownhound wanes alwaysopen
    lookingeyes restingwondering
  so he shufllesstyles away slow indifferent performatively
    unphasedetached
  and mopmutt hollers chainchoked parched throatchain
    stuckbuckled
  and brownhound tilts cornrice masheddressed snout left
    right eyes slowaiting

  and maybeukenglish caucasian male miles from homeland
haven
  and hand hair voice wallopwail wallopail walopail
    waopail and serviettes sail flailinggloatingfloating
flailgfloating   flailgloafloating flailgfloating
flaiflailfloating
  and people jumpsurround reachretain
  and doublenosering big blackbooted plaidpants hair
    dredded to achilles maybe ukenglish maybe
    familyman caucasian male cinematic
    pacinonicholson pontificates Are you calling me a
bastard Do you know what that means Do you   know
what that means Ill have your job

  and midsize brownhound humble staringtilting blueyes
    parched yapping mopmutt almost screeching
    pascals wager and maximum utility and leap of   faith
  and eternal recurrence and categorical   imperative and
hammerness
  and brownhound bear snout hollers hellhello
  and oldmop smallstretcheschokes yoganeck attack
  but chance at changeredemption suddenow slimnarrow
    as brownhound snapbitestrangles loudfast fangs
    locked   awaiting slimnarrow survivalsurrender

refrain

and caucasian doublenosering singlelipring female sits
silentalonesome onebeer onecigarette in onehand
browneyes tearpooled heavyface halftryinghiding
and caucasian long kneelunging dreddedhair
doublenosering male aims intentionvoice
outsidedoors to settle argumenthings
and then Call manager and then Call police and then Call
manager
and then Call manager police manager settlethings
serious around corner past door down stairs   through
hallway beyond exitoutside
and customers employees custodians surroundstill shifty
arms to stopstifle preemptive furiousflailing fists
and friendly probablylocal drunk cigarsmoking man sits
alongside wetcheeked doublenosering onelipring
onebeer onecigarette palefemale
explainingrefraining away tearstroubles
and still stolidstrong plaidpanted blackbooted
foreverhaired maybebritish male exhales stoic
Manager on the phone now

and mopmutt agonizedailing brownhounds jawclench
seizing solid
but bigbluebeiged schooluniform boys answer mopmutts
chainchoked jawtrapped weakening whitelight   cry
hungryhounds prepostpubescent ribs   rerecracked

and drunk smoking friendlyfrankind indian gentlemans
fortyplus overweight frame bloated
leaningreachinggrasping leanreachgrasping over table at
tripleringpierced females facespace horrified and
white chair tiltfalls sideways
and darksuited darkhaired darkeyed friendassociate
indian quickpullsrestrains indian nevergentleman
and lipringed female shiversconvulses mouthmoving He
asked if need sex Sex

refrain

and you
you

and drunksmoking unfriendly ungentleman
    pulledpushedcrushed pullpushcrushed to original
    seat original table original asscociatesfriends
    original remove

and too many moviehouses hollywood hopes

and plaidpanted blackbooted doublenoseringed dredded
    deadhair and Missed service Missed managers   and
Ill have your job
and misses female onelipring hollywood seenscene and
    mockheroic maybeukenglish bangs bigbill on
    romantic bighouse register

and mopmutts now olderbluer eyes begbeckon
    whinewhimpering attention attraction devotion   desire
and ribcracked brownhound sixhand held

and it keeps on beginning

refrain

smile momentarily answers

smile momentarily answers another marriage quest
her shivershock

and on to gangtok
and redtape seas
and clocks laughing

jumpyjammed jeepride real
and worth the trip
pirsigs zen thumbsup
road winding ayeaye rumblerumbletumble
signs sing silently

Speed thrills but kills
Blow horn at every turn
Always alert accidents avert
and sikkim state alive
and tourist office offers
and affluent man takes prejudice precedence

dirtyclad swollenfaced stutteredmuttered
    stammeredslurred blackeyed blackbelt blackboots
    other forbiddengotten
so lotus hotel
warm red rugs
big overcast view
hotwater everlasting
and capital steppes streeted
foreverhaired woman cautiously scopedconsumed

and no maiden mirrored in a cursed spell
and blue ribbon brandy thins blood and wideopens libido
    eyes
and magazine elbow rests relaxed on plastic table as left

refrain

    hand cradles hidden ear and endlessly enshawled
    head halfconceals unreadable smile
    enframedbordered by bigmouthlips
and her eyes clutchclimb deep
and you retreatlook within as she knowingly
    decommands
almond harp halo still subtle eyes never blinking looking
    staring giving inging back
only taking

and siddhartha renounced renouncing samana at sight
    smell whisperwish kamala
and mind races paces faces
and dh lawrence is dead
and thoughts drink stagnant still
starving raving craving for crushing slushing source

refrain

casual meander slow

casual meander slow uphill wander
past touchedtackledtrampled thamel square hotels shops
    pushers takers
around alley bend green mountains more everywhere
single sparse clouds streak oceandark sky building what
    your mind will

and monkey temple yells loud prayer flags
and budding bodhi trees
and growing foothills
and steps steps steps hundreds up

stupa bigger foothills greenersteeper
more profound silent sound
and beads carved rock wood buddhas
handmade masks shiny silver bracelets

swords icecream scarves sashes sarees hats stone crystal
    gold glass
and temple grows with heart rate
and Hail to the jewel in the lotus
hand touchturning 108 prayerwheels right to left

and cameras frame redbrick mass metropolis below
green greener mountains caught in white
and thoreau whispers something in whitmans longone
    song
and monkeys are quick crazed violent

refrain

tibetan monk fasthands neverending banknotes
and his pepsi halfempty not halfull
and lotus assumed old lady brings back holiness
not knowing showing a this worldly material thing

its all desire and suffering
cameras capturing very most least of it
and buddha gifts warm butterfly fuzzy unfeeling
and the cafe de stupa emptyhollow packed to the gills

and not even zen could laugh it away

refrain

buddhist beads explain

buddhist beads explain hair away
and barbers bone cracking crunching rock reaping
    knuckle lead fist cranium cracking
so pounding head bulging pushout or pullin struggling
    striving eyebulbs

and jeep charts jetblack smoketoke trail
misty mountain clouds hugging loving
waterfalls wail peaceful paceful clear cold

hard heavy olderthanwind rock
and sun screams Namaskar
stillife shadows stand staring

road a twisting trail climb plunge bump
and monkeys rest remembering
while leaves colour themselves absent

and head hollers help
pain pushing emptying eyes
maniacal migrained maligned mind

and gange gorge guards longstumbling stones
rustyredyellowbrown leaf cushy cloud collision
and golden dawn awesome oranges at ten am

and pelling crest cradles distant snows
as hawks wheel on fortunes right
agni glides behind rock and hawk paling orange yellow
    black

refrain

bigbear hugging view
and merciless migraine pain
blinding whitelight internal infernal forever fever

but sweet dawn
and jeep jumps descending
eyes abused confused

eon eon eon
ailing eyes answerbegging
and ceiling fan spins once a minute

and denton doctors devastation starvation
eyes abandoning futile pushpull
and silly siliguri sings escape

and rickshaw bustand inevitable irritable wardingwaving
travel agents jeep drivers reaching wallahs pestering
    pedestrians
telling yelling time patience youth

and twist tug busboard bend
and still no textbook lushplush brahmin perfect palace
and checkstop passport forms photos greenbacks

and dipsomaniac details katmandu days
and he needs drink like fire a better chariot than sun
bugswat buswait as oneeyed spot hound rocktossed
    stickstung

and tea stall girls slap away holy holycows
and two dacoits will clash knuckles trade fistfits
sannyasis levitate unburdened unbeckoned by

refrain

stone dodge hotspot hound pickchews reeking rubbish
and tourists dusttrack big packs backs
stoop man cackles awake lighting cough brown beedi

and water buffalo walkrots away
Nai bus we have Already and Nai rickshaw
and lazy bus laughs leaving marvell long later

and wood stockpiled on ricketyrackety roof
tightsqueeze aisle bodystuck mind breaking
and no ultraviolet vision to read night away

and dream of dreams dream delivered
and transmissions sisyphus screechclimb overrules rest
and palas athene summons dawn golden growing sky

and beer signs breathe katmandu call
and slushing fountain carpet room white towels
and bookstores store stores of books

and Opiumhash Changemoney
breathe sigh drink swallow smile
and comfort controls

and that limits

refrain

refrain

air india announces

air india announces direct delhilondon takeoff in three
    thinning dwindling days
so its a five am doghowl hurried upcall in snowcapped
    cold katmandu
stars resting blanketing

sun climbs clouds dreaming
foothills breathe greener
rice fields realer than lofty wedding cakes

and bus dusts midday mist
white distance himalaya inhales
breasts bounce bustling grandma smiles

and pokhara permits ponder room

and bus aboard rebeginsumes
bright punjabied girls trailside hillside all smiles
nosering gracing all holifestival coveredcoloured

and kesey bustop untrimmed trees weave
and blueyes dravidian souls
soaking suns crimson stroke green treetops fasting
    clouds

and big dipper sevens
drunken delhi dancers loud paintslamming
big balloons bombard passerby holi

and darting donkey zebrablackwhite specklespot hounds
room candle forgetting the dark difference
so perspective changes

refrain

refrain

as sure as

as sure as planes will grow in comfort and cleanliness
    tenfold in indian arrivaldeparture interim
and as sure as rainbows have cartoon beginnings
and stars conspire to steal the sky
the romantic ideal rarely intersects indias real

as turbulence troubled planes giratedly jump less than
    delhis dubious buildings on buildings crookedly
        struggling suffering through shadows
up up kissing smiling sun
like laughing lotus flowers unsoiled lifelunge

like don juan desired deeper delving
and siddharthas lotus limbed renouncing fasting forgetting
long unwashed unkept falling out hair   ribs poking fullout
eyes plunging fullin   unstriving for fullemptied flame

and avolokitesvara wishes for alls unwishing
and amitabha laughs loud lazy long luminescence
simon gracefully mileaged and middleaged nam vet   army
hair veering verystrong left
dragon tattoo fanning flaming left forearm

and simon proves that paradox unbuilds previously   sound
blocks that questiondoubt divergent reason
that futures past blows horns outside in
that shadows retire too much touched
as he sits doublefisting cigarette and blackest stone

refrain

and thinks of neverful ashtrays
talking of several scattered sons and kashmiri carpets
and his endless knowing all to well for he met His
    holiness the dalai lama today and he commends   Thai
stick

and Thailand sex is very fair
and his satellite dish is being installed
and dharamsala will soon sell cellular phone service
and Technology is good
Global westernization is bad

and Buddhism is his business
and he commends yani
and defames distrusted inlaws who made him miss Yanis
    show at the Fucking fabulous taj temple mahal   and
he Cant forget forgive

and Srinigar is fine
barely twenty assassinations last night
and mcdonalds mcmutton Burgers fresh
and he avoids All garbage food
and You might not know this But ive been recognized by
    the dalai lama His holiness himself

so I adorn the robes next month
and he elaborates on his la monastery
and weekends in sleepless spain
and his house at everest base camp one
and doesnt mind altitude

refrain

and patience has evolved radical in past twenty years
but needs Thermal glass doubleplated windows at sure
    soon nepali western home
and must have Jetstream six foot by eight green jacuzzi
and sherpas will swing the fragile fiberglass deadweight

and Plumbings all worked out
and his cigarettes in empty coke
and he takes a rickshaw five blocks
so kashmiri friend can buy him shirts trousers time life
    fuck luck longing

now simon sits johnny walker special in hand
raving about connoisseur quality manali pot
Grows as free as dandelions in mad america
and 500 us should be plenty for ten days in katmandu
and his flights only 280 round trip

and No way hes gracing the thirtysix hour bus
and his crystal glass empties
as his cigarette filters away
so his mouth finally shuts
and his eyes must follow

and
we all want
until time
no longer lies
waiting

refrain

refrain

THE PUBLISHERS

Proverse Hong Kong (PVHK), founded by Gillian and Verner Bickley, is based in Hong Kong with long-term and developing regional and international connections.

We have published novels, novellas, non-fiction (including autobiography and biography, history, memoirs, sport, travel narratives), single-author poetry collections, children's, young teens and academic books. Other interests include diaries, and academic works in the humanities, social sciences, cultural studies, linguistics and education. Some Proverse books have accompanying audio texts. Some are translated into Chinese.

We welcome authors who have a story to tell, wisdom, perceptions or information to convey, a person they want to memorialize, a neglect they want to remedy, a record they want to correct, a strong interest that they want to share, skills they want to teach, and who consciously seek to make a contribution to society in an informative, interesting and well-written way. Proverse works with texts by non-native-speaker writers of English as well as by native English-speaking writers.

The name, "Proverse", combines the words "prose" and "verse" and is pronounced accordingly.

refrain

THE INTERNATIONAL PROVERSE PRIZE FOR UNPUBLISHED BOOK-LENGTH FICTION, NON-FICTION OR POETRY

The Proverse Prize, an annual international competition for an unpublished single-author book-length work of fiction, non-fiction, or poetry, the original work of the entrant, submitted in English (translations welcomed) was established in January 2008. It is open to all who are at least eighteen on the date they sign the entry form and without restriction of nationality, residence or citizenship.

Founded by Gillian and Verner Bickley, the objectives of the prize are: to encourage excellence and / or excellence and usefulness in publishable written work in the English Language, which can, in varying degrees, "delight and instruct". Entries are invited from anywhere in the world.

The Prize
1) Publication by Proverse Hong Kong, with
2) Cash prize of HKD10,000 (HKD7.80 = approx. USD1.00)

Extent of the Manuscript: within the range of what is usual for the genre of the work submitted. However, it is advisable that novellas be in the range, 30,000 to 45,000 words; other fiction (e.g. novels, short-story collections) and non-fiction (e.g. autobiographies, biographies, diaries, letters, memoirs, essay collections, etc.) should be in the range, 75,000 to 100,000 words. Poetry collections should be in the range, 5,000 to 25,000 words. Other word-counts and mixed-genre submissions are not ruled out.

Annual Entry Deadlines (subject to confirmation and/or change)

Receipt of Entry Fees / Entry Forms begins	[Variable, no later than] 14 April
Deadline for receipt of Entry Fees / Entry Forms	31 May
Receipt of entered manuscripts begins	1 May
Deadline for receipt of entered manuscripts	30 June

More information, updated from time to time, is available on the Proverse website: proversepublishing.com

refrain

THE INTERNATIONAL PROVERSE POETRY PRIZE (SINGLE POEMS)

An annual international Proverse Poetry Prize (for single poems) was established in 2016. The international Proverse Poetry Prize is open to all who are at least eighteen years old whatever their residence, nationality or citizenship.
Single poems, submitted in English, are invited on (a) <u>any subject or theme, chosen by the writer</u> OR (b) <u>on a subject or theme selected by the organisers</u>.
Poems may be in any form, style or genre. Each poem should be no more than 30 lines.
Entries should previously be unpublished in any way (except in the case of unpublished translations into English of the entrant's own work already published in another language, providing the entrant holds the copyright).
Entrants keep their copyright.

**In 2016
cash prizes were offered as follows:
1st prize; USD100.00; 2nd prize: USD45.00;
3rd prizes (up to four winners): USD20.00.**

If there are enough good entries in any year, an anthology of prize-winners and selected other entries will be published.
In 2016, judging took place at the same time as the judging for the Proverse Prize for unpublished book-length fiction, non-fiction or poetry.
Judges: anonymous (as for the Proverse Prize for an unpublished book-length work).
Max number of entries per person: No maximum.
No poet may win more than one prize.

**The above information is for guidance only.
More information, updated from time to time, is available on the Proverse website: proversepublishing.com**

refrain

POETRY PUBLISHED BY PROVERSE

Those who enjoy **refrain** may also enjoy the following.

Alphabet, by Andrew S Guthrie, 2014.

Astra and Sebastian, by L.W. Illsley. 2011.

Chasing Light, by Patricia Glinton-Meicholas. 2013.

China suite and other poems, by Gillian Bickley. 2009.

For the record and other poems of Hong Kong, by Gillian Bickley. 2003.

Freda Kahlo's Cry and Other Poems, by Laura Solomon, 2015.

Heart to Heart, by Patty Ho, 2010.

Home, away, elsewhere, by Vaughan Rapatahana. 2011.

Immortelle and bhandaaraa poems, by Lelawattee Manoo-Rahming. 2011.

In vitro, by Laura Solomon. 2nd ed., 2014.

Irreverent Poems for Pretentious People, by Henrik Hoeg, 2016.

Life Lines, by Shahilla Shariff, 2012.

Moving house and other poems from Hong Kong, by Gillian Bickley. 2005.

Of Leaves and Ashes, by Patty Ho, 2016.

Of symbols misused by Mary-Jane Newton. March 2011.

Painting the borrowed house: poems, by Kate Rogers. 2008.

Perceptions, by Gillian Bickley. 2012.

Rain on the Pacific Coast, by Elbert Siu Ping Lee, 2013.

refrain

refrain, by Jason S. Polley. 2010.

Shadow play, by James Norcliffe. 2012.

Shadows in Deferment, by Birgit Linder. 2013.

Shifting Sands, by Deepa Vanjani, 2016.

Sightings, by Gillian Bickley. 2007.

Smoked pearl: poems of Hong Kong and beyond, by Akin Jeje (Akinsola Olufemi Jeje). 2010.

The Layers Between, by Celia Claase, 2015.

Unlocking, by Mary-Jane Newton, 2014.

Wonder, lust & itchy feet, by Sally Dellow. 2011.

POETRY – CHINESE LANGUAGE

For the record and other poems of Hong Kong, by Gillian Bickley. Translated by Simon Chow. 2010. E-bk.

Moving house and other poems from Hong Kong, translated into chinese, with additional material, by Gillian Bickley. Edited by Tony Ming-Tak Yip. Translated by Tony Yip and others. 2008.

~~~

refrain

FIND OUT MORE ABOUT OUR AUTHORS BOOKS AND EVENTS

Visit our website:
http://www.proversepublishing.com

Visit our distributor's website: <www.chineseupress.com>

Follow us on Twitter
Follow news and conversation: twitter.com/Proversebooks>
OR
Copy and paste the following to your browser window and follow the instructions:
https://twitter.com/#!/ProverseBooks

"Like" us on www.facebook.com/ProversePress

Request our free E-Newsletter
Send your request to info@proversepublishing.com.

Availability
Most books are available in Hong Kong and world-wide
from our Hong Kong based Distributor,
The Chinese University Press of Hong Kong,
The Chinese University of Hong Kong, Shatin, NT,
Hong Kong SAR, China.
Email: cup-bus@cuhk.edu.hk
Website: <www.chineseupress.com>.

All titles are available from Proverse Hong Kong
http://www.proversepublishing.com

and the Proverse Hong Kong UK-based Distributor.

We have **stock-holding retailers** in Hong Kong,
Singapore (Select Books),
Canada (Elizabeth Campbell Books),
Andorra (Llibreria La Puça, La Llibreria).
Orders can be made from bookshops in the UK and elsewhere.

Ebooks
Most of our titles are available also as Ebooks.

www.ingramcontent.com/pod-product-compliance
Lightning Source LLC
Chambersburg PA
CBHW062121080426
42734CB00012B/2944